Zendaya
Disney Channel Actress

by Lucas Diver

ABDO
POP BIOS
Kids

abdopublishing.com

Published by Abdo Kids, a division of ABDO, PO Box 398166, Minneapolis, Minnesota 55439.

Copyright © 2015 by Abdo Consulting Group, Inc. International copyrights reserved in all countries. No part of this book may be reproduced in any form without written permission from the publisher.

Printed in the United States of America, North Mankato, Minnesota.

102014

012015

 THIS BOOK CONTAINS RECYCLED MATERIALS

Photo Credits: AP Images, Corbis, iStock

Production Contributors: Teddy Borth, Jennie Forsberg, Grace Hansen

Design Contributors: Laura Rask, Dorothy Toth

Library of Congress Control Number: 2014943784

Cataloging-in-Publication Data

Diver, Lucas.

 Zendaya: Disney Channel actress / Lucas Diver.

  p. cm. -- (Pop bios)

Includes index.

ISBN 978-1-62970-729-7

1. Zendaya, 1996- --Juvenile literature. 2. Actors--United States--Biography--Juvenile literature. 3. Singers--United States--Biography--Juvenile literature. 4. Models (Persons)--United States--Biography--Juvenile literature. 1. Title.

791.4302--dc23

[B]

2014943784

Table of Contents

Birth & Childhood

Zendaya Coleman was born
on September 1, 1996. She
was born in Oakland, California.

5

Her mother was a **house manager** at a local theater. Zendaya helped at the theater.

Zendaya loved to act. She also loved to sing and dance.

Shake It Up

In 2009, Zendaya **auditioned** for *Shake It Up*. She landed the role of Rocky Blue.

Shake It Up **debuted** in 2010.

It is an original Disney series.

Bella Thorne and Zendaya costar
on the show.

13

Singer & Dancer

In 2012, Zendaya signed a record deal. She released the single "Replay" in 2013.

15

Zendaya was on *Dancing with the Stars* in 2013. She made it to the finals. She got second place!

K.C. Undercover

Disney's *K.C. Undercover* shot a **pilot** in early 2014. Filming was set to begin in early 2015. Zendaya had the **lead**.

19

What's Next?

Zendaya sings, acts, and so much more. What will she amaze fans with next?

21

Timeline

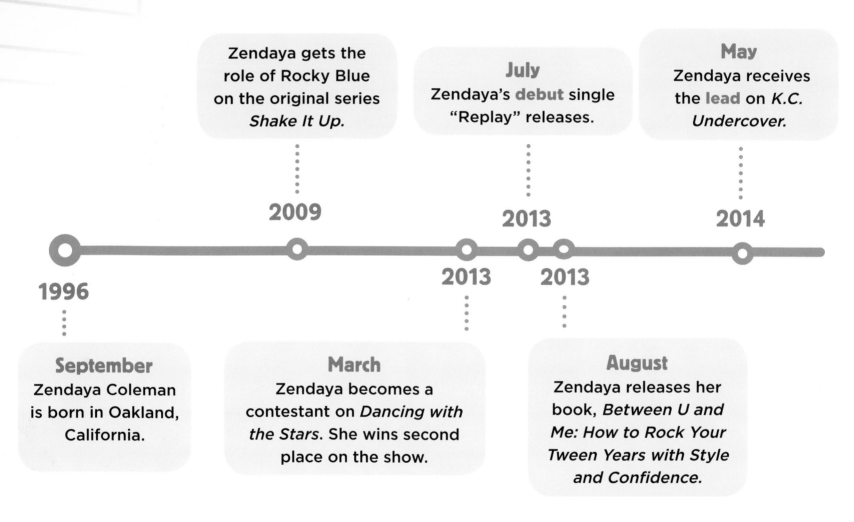

Zendaya gets the role of Rocky Blue on the original series *Shake It Up*.

July
Zendaya's **debut** single "Replay" releases.

May
Zendaya receives the **lead** on *K.C. Undercover*.

2009

2013

2014

1996

2013

2013

September
Zendaya Coleman is born in Oakland, California.

March
Zendaya becomes a contestant on *Dancing with the Stars*. She wins second place on the show.

August
Zendaya releases her book, *Between U and Me: How to Rock Your Tween Years with Style and Confidence*.

Glossary

audition – to try out for a part in a play, movie, or television show.

debut – to show to the public for the first time.

house manager – someone who is responsible for managing a theater and its staff.

lead – the person who plays the main character in a show.

pilot – one episode made as a test to see if a television series will be successful.

23

Index

abdokids.com

Use this code to log on to abdokids.com and access crafts, games, videos, and more!

Abdo Kids Code:
PZK7297